ELLA

A Baby Elephant's Story

Executive Producers, John Christianson and Ron Berry
Illustrator, Lara Gurin
Art Director and Book Designer, Eugene Epstein
Writer and Creative Director, Kathleen Duey
DVD Mastering and Editor, Stephanie Carlson
DVD Soundtrack and Song Composed and Produced by George Fogelman
DVD Audio Mixed and Mastered by Robert Cartwright and George Fogelman
DVD Video Narrator, Erin Ashe
DVD Song, Sung by Erin Ashe, Ian Brininstool, Alexa Bergman, Danny Myers, Rebecca Myers,
DVD Video Footage, the British Broadcasting Company
Production Manager, Doug Boggs

Distributed by Ideals Publications
A Guideposts Company
535 Metroplex Drive, Nashville, TN 37211

ISBN 978-0-8249-5584-7
Printed and bound in China

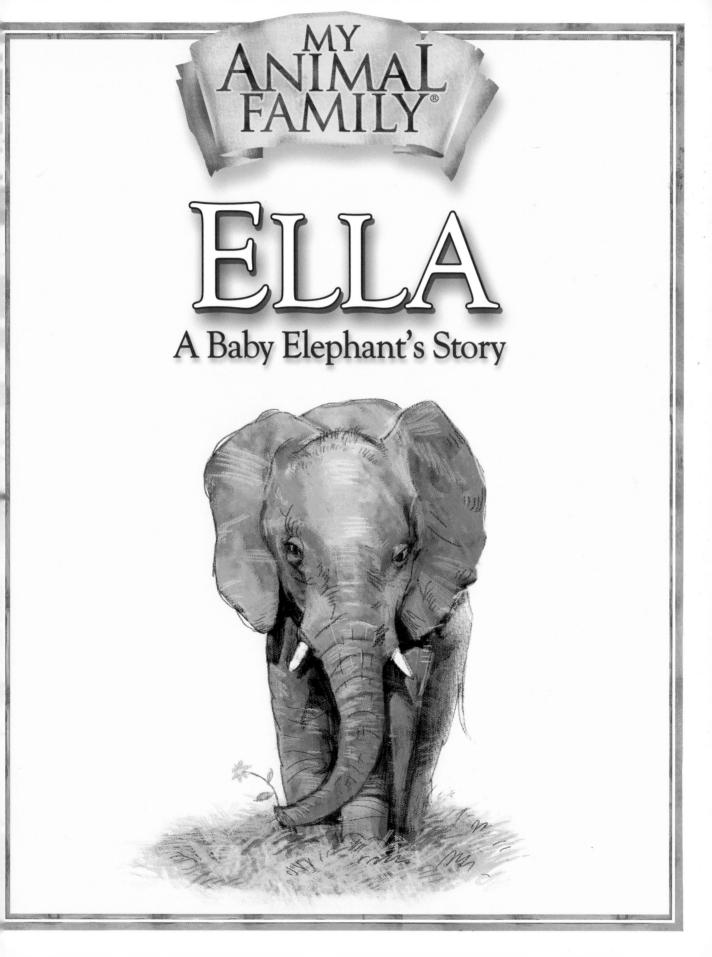

MY ANIMAL FAMILY®

ELLA

A Baby Elephant's Story

*I*t had rained most of the night. My mother and I were still sleepy.

My aunt was near us, still asleep. She would soon have her first baby.

I heard my mother sigh. Then I heard something else.

Not with my ears—this was a sound that came from far away

through the damp earth beneath my feet.

I knew what it meant. Visitors!

My grandmother was the first to lift her trunk and trumpet.

My older brother stared into the distance—we all watched

the horizon. Finally, we saw my father's herd coming toward us.

Grandmother led us to greet them.

Elephants always love to visit with family and friends.

My mother was so glad to see my father and my two oldest

brothers. They are big now—they're almost grown up.

My father is so BIG! Every time I see him, he lets me

follow him while he digs up grass with his tusks.

Elephants have to eat a lot. Once the grass is gone

wherever we are, we have to travel to find more.

So before long, my father's herd had to leave again.

We all trumpeted goodbye. Then my grandmother

started walking and we all followed her.

We were hungry, too!

A few days later, one of my aunts was swaying,
lifting her trunk high, then lowering it again.
That meant she was going to have a baby soon.
My cousins and I stayed close to her—but not too close.
We didn't want to bother her. We were just excited.

The next night, the baby was born.

When the sun came up, we all stamped and trumpeted

and welcomed the newborn into the herd.

The baby looked so little to me.

I was much bigger than she was.

A few days later, my aunt let me touch the baby.

She was very shy. Her little trunk swung back and forth.

I was careful not to startle her.

As the days passed, my aunt didn't mind at all if her baby followed me around. It was fun! I was very careful. I made sure she didn't get into any trouble.

Watching the baby try to use her trunk, I realized how much I had learned. She couldn't pull up her own grass yet so I let her have some of mine.

I tried to help her practice every single day, like my brother had helped me.

One night we heard hyenas barking in the darkness.

I wasn't afraid. They are dangerous for baby elephants,

but so long as the whole herd is close, they are afraid of us.

My mother lay awake, but I went back to sleep.

The next day, my grandmother led us eastward, toward the river.

My aunt seemed tired. Maybe the hyenas had kept her awake.

She dropped back to the end of the line. I walked with her and her baby.

Halfway to the river, we all stopped because a storm was rising.

It rained hard that night. It scared the baby a little.

It was her first rainstorm. She stood very close to me.

The day after the rain was sunny and hot.

So when we got to the river, my mother and most of

the herd waded into the water. My aunt found a place

to doze in the shade while her baby followed me into the shallows.

*A*fter we got out of the water, the baby and I
played hide and seek in the tall grass. Then I tried to teach her
how to pull it up by the roots.

I was hungry! For a long time she stayed close and watched me eat.

So I didn't notice when she walked back toward the river.

When I looked up, I couldn't see her.

I scented hyenas and ran into the trees.

I found her trembling in a little clearing in the trees.

I was scared, too. The hyenas were so close!

Stamping my feet, I made a low, rumbling sound that

I knew my mother would hear—and she did!

I heard her loud, strong trumpet, and then my grandmother's.

I hoped they would come fast. The biggest hyena growled.

I was so scared. But I knew what I had to do. I charged the hyenas—then I heard my mother and the rest of the herd right behind me!

The ground shook as my family thundered into the clearing.

The hyenas all ran!

I was so glad that the baby was safe.

Everyone was. My mother was so proud of me.

I saw my grandmother calming everyone as we

walked across the wide grasslands. I watched her.

Maybe someday, I would be the one leading the herd.

We all slept close together that night,

in a meadow far from the river.

The moon was bright. I knew my mother

and grandmother would keep watch for danger.

So I closed my eyes and went to sleep,

breathing the familiar scents of grass and warm earth,

listening to the sleepy sounds of my big family.

The Illustrated Book

Our picture books are written with care and beautifully illustrated.
Every story is about the realistic adventures of a baby wild animal,
an accurate portrayal shaped by current behavioral research.
Each story gives parents and grandparents opportunities to talk to
their children about life, home, and family.

The Activity Website

The **My Animal Family** creative team includes game and website designers, too. We have built a **safe**, fun place for kids to play "animal" activities online. At **MAFKidsClub.com**, children will find their favorite animal friends in their native habitats. Set in arctic snow, tropical forests, oceans and deserts, the games help pre-readers get ready for school and keep beginning readers happy and busy. Games are leveled so that each visitor can build confidence and master basic skills. The creative team has worked hard to make the website friendly, fun, interesting and safe for your kids.

The Live-Action Animal DVD

Every book includes a live-action DVD that features **award-winning BBC** wildlife video footage. Carefully edited for young children, the footage gives them a glimpse into the reality of each baby animal's life. Kids learn about the cooperation that helps animal families survive and thrive, and about the habitats they live in.

LEO — *A Baby Lion's Story*

Leo goes exploring, then has to find his way back to his family

KOROW — *Baby Chimpanzee's Story*

Korow learns to climb high enough to pick her own fruit.

ELLA — *A Baby Elephant's Story*

Ella helps protect a newborn baby elephant in danger.

NANUQ — *A Baby Polar Bear's Story*

Nanuq saves his bossy brother from a foolish mistake.

MY ANIMAL FAMILY®

Welcome to the Club!

My Animal Family is a new kind of children's club. With books to read, DVDs to enjoy, games to play, puzzles to solve and adventures to share, it's the kind of club every child dreams of... *"where the fun and good times never stop."*

Membership begins with the purchase of a beautifully illustrated storybook. Every story in the series is captivating and stars a baby animal in a realistic, family adventure... animal families that include elephants, lions, chimpanzees, polar bears, and many more...

Use the secret passcode on your membership card to explore *www.MAFKidsClub.com*
There are no advertisements or fees